Set Your Wild Heart Free

Heather Picardat

Presentation by *BookLeaf Publishing*

Web: www.bookleafpub.com

E-mail: info@bookleafpub.com

ISBN: 9789357615860

First edition 2023

DEDICATION

This one is for anyone who took a moment to really understand themselves, and those who still need to.

Bloom

Bloom where you are planted
Let your wild heart grow
There is beauty in your soul
In everything you touch

You were born to blossom
Your aura destined to glow
You were meant to be something
Much more than you know

Bloom where you are planted
Flourish and shine
Your light is the beacon
In somebody's eyes

You're almost ready to sprout
Your mind is gold
Turn and face the sun
Let your spirit be bold

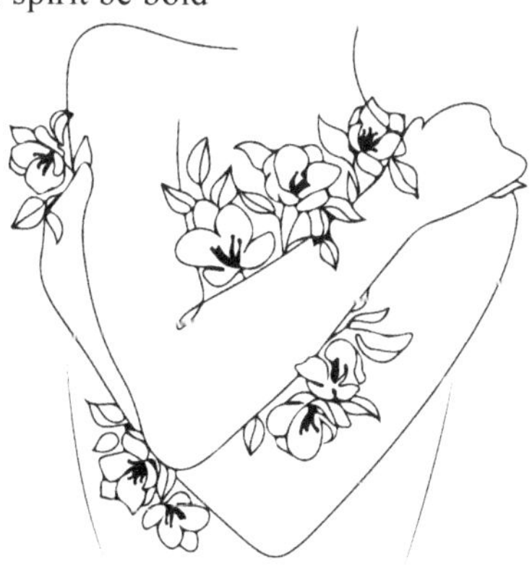

Drowning

2

When I dive in
Unafraid of the depth
I sometimes forget
I don't know how to swim
Down I sink
Chest full
Waves crashing
Down down down
Until I feel nothing

Deeply Rooted

Some find it so easy
To come and go
Relationships are temporary
Friendships, menial

But me... I think I'm cursed
My loyalty is deeply rooted
I grasp onto any
Meaningful connection I can reach
And attach myself lovingly

I long for connection
Crave the admiration
Shower them in attention
Often too much attention
Squeezing the life right out of them

Leaching away all that's good
Until eventually they leave me
They always do
And I sulk in my rotted roots
For another season

Delicate

Not all flowers are delicate
Sometimes the most beautiful things
Can still be poison

You were the hemlock
In a cluster of fennel
You were moonseed
In Martha's Vineyard
You were nightshade
In a blueberry pie

How deceptive
The most beautiful
delicate things

Summer of 99

Lilac and puce
Clouds floating
Through the deep ocean
Speckled sky
Like fluffy bites
Of cotton candy
We used to eat
When we were young

My favorite shade
Of sunset
My favorite feeling
Careless, Happy, Free
Such a shame to only
Remember these things
In the Indian summers

Remember the state fair?
Remember barefoot bike rides?
Remember just come home
When the street lights turn on?

Now we're plucking
Cotton candy from the sky
Wishing to relive
Those summer nights

Hey There

Hey there baby boy
Tiny wondrous bitty boy
Hey my sweet reflection
All the best parts of me

Hey there balled up baby fists
All the strength I thought I needed
Hey there dew drop honey eyes
Full of innocence and awe

Hey soft sweet snuggle bug
My second heart beating
I loved you from the second
I heard yours in rhythm to mine

Hey there baby boy
My first littlest love
My bundle of sunshine
The best new beginning

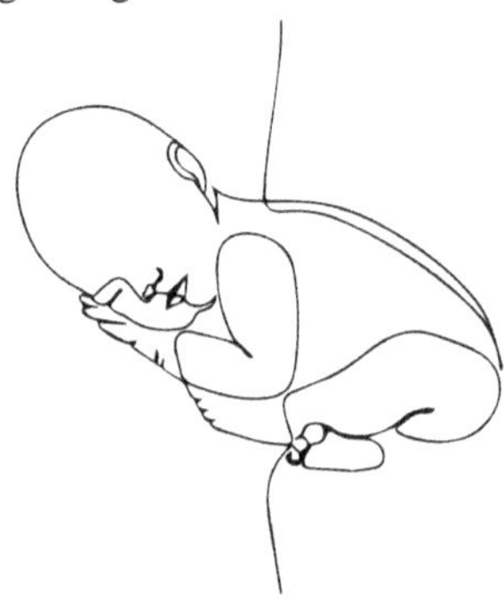

Growing Pains

Growing is slow and painful
But necessary and rewarding
Nothing worth doing has ever been
Made easy
And that's the journey you see
Its the baby steps
That matter most, that get you there
To climb the mountain carefully
Feeling for the right hand-space
To make the hike steadily
Pushing one foot at a time
To stretch the cloth precisely
Around each bend and curve
It's not the volume of the work
It's not the swiftness
It's the dedication
The assertion... The absolute rigor
Yes growing is slow and painful
But it's invigorating and rewarding

Shine

Treasure those who treasure you
You shine in radiating friendships
That regard you as the light
That you are
Who you've always been
If you're not all shining
Then none of you are
Everyone has a light
We all deserve to be ignited
Grant yourself at least that much

Learning to Swim

9

If 71% of what we know
Is merely ocean
Vast and blue
If 95% of our world is water
Is endless and mysterious
And we've spent all our time
Searching for happiness
On these same pieces of land
With no promise
We really ought to
Venture out
Dive in
And learn to swim

No good for me

I'm addicted to
An unfaithful specimen
Anyone likely to
Tell me lies
Foolish enough to
Keep believing them
To keep holding onto
Precious words
Because they sound good
So attracted to
The garbage way
I'm always being
Walked all over
Anyone who makes a promise
But bends and breaks it
Who commits to a good time
And cancels at the last minute
Those are my people
I'm just a glutton for punishment

Kids

Kids are so good
At storytelling
Imagine- they say
Imagine
And they intertwine
Real life and fantasy
Into therapeutic musings
Clever little beings

Settle for less

Conditioned to feel insignificant
I spent my whole life
Believing I'm not good enough

She will never be beautiful
She will never be smart
She will never make friends
She will never amount to anything

And I guess some of it is true
But I have tenancy to prove
Everyone wrong

I never recognize my worth
Until it begins to fade
Never understanding my appeal
Until it's long gone
I try so hard to be a people pleaser
That I forget to please myself

Celebrating any attention
That makes me feel seen
And then I settle for less
Assuming it will bring me happiness
I haven't felt happiness yet

Love

I don't doubt that you loved me
One time you did
Your eyes told me
Your mouth upon mine
Your body told me
The goosebumps on your skin
Our fingers locked
Our legs touching beneath blankets
Bodies longing for warmth
Reaching for acceptance
Bodies craving serotonin
Breathing in each other's scent
Hearts racing, racing, racing...
Until they stopped caring
Slowly descending from one another
I don't doubt that you loved me
One time I know you did
But you stopped loving yourself
And we slipped away

Clean

Something doesn't feel right anymore
This place is unclean

Where I used to burrow in rosewater
All that pools is septic
Where I used to bathe in lavender and prim
Now smeared with thick black mold

Where once I was hugged in soft fresh cotton
I'm suffocating in cyanide
Where once I was basked in verbena white tea
I'm now engulfed by clouds of soot

I'd scrub my whole body
Until my skin falls off
Just to feel that clean again

The Millennial Dilemma

This generation is so alone
Our village is an abandoned town
Remember Grandma's house
Every week, all summer?

Now we're begging for a night away
Remember auntie's cabin on the lake?
Cousins were our first best friends
These kids are lucky if they
Even have cousins at all
Our families are broken and incomplete

We don't travel like we used to
We don't get to know each other
Grandpa's solution is a dollar bill
When all they need is some quality time

We don't even know the neighbors by name
The neighborhood kids don't come over to play
We keep to ourselves
We've stopped asking for help
We don't know how to make friends
Or keep the ones we've got
There's no village anymore

Choose Happy

Choose happy
As if it were a choice
As if you choose to hate yourself
Choose to wallow
Choose to cry
Choose to barely get out of bed
Choose to medicate
So you can choose to make it through another day
alive

As if you could just choose
To wake up one morning
Throw a smile on your face
Embrace the day
And just decide that now
On this day that you've chosen
And poof
Now you're happy
So glad you've made the choice

Morning Glory

Like any good perennial
I've circumvented
Any possibility of
Simply ceasing to exist
Just call me Morning Glory
I'll be here spreading
My wildflowers
Summoning the bees
Wrapping my vines
Until I feel seen

Two birds

Two birds meet
Beneath a willow tree
Their vibrant wings
Spread wide against
Mossy green
Two birds majestically
Singing melody
Their song echoing
From branch to branch
Two birds weaving
Twigs and leaves to nest
Drinking Hector from the flowers
Laying baby chicks to rest
Two birds flying wistfully
Happily as can be
Leaning only on each other
If two birds were you and me

Serotonin

19

Buy the serotonin
To make you feel better
To grasp onto
A sliver of happiness
Just enough to feel normal

Get so used to
Simply living
You forget what it means
To feel like dying
So if you run out
You can start all over again

Bend and Break

I'm bending to fit the mold
Make myself flexible enough
To seem rounded
I've got all the time in the world

Rearrange my schedule
Spend my money
Drive my car all over town
Put this need above my own
Set myself on the sideline
Assume the favor is appreciated

But when I need an ear
Someone to lean on
A helping hand
Nobody is bending for me

Wither like the Autumn

I've always loved the autumn
The moody hues and fiery tones
I love the breeze
The whistling wind
The hazy sunset
The harvest moon
Most of all I love the flora
The changing leaves
The dewy morning glow
The comfort of knowing
That rest is coming
Dormant until the next era
The chance to fade and start again
Autumnal energy in full effect